Also by John Sager

A Tiffany Monday – an Unusual Love Story, West

Joan's Gallery, 50 Years of Artistry by Joan Johns

Uncovered – My Half-Century with the CIA, West Bow Press 2013

Night Flight, A Novel, Create Space, 2013

Operation Night Hawk, A Novel, Create Space, 2014

Moscow at Midnight, A Novel, Create Space, 2014

The Jihadists' Revenge, A Novel, Create Space, 2014

Mole, A Novel, Create Space, 2015

Capital Crises, A Novel, Create Space, 2015

God's Listeners, An Anthology, Create Space, 2015

Crescent Blood, A Novel, Create Space 2016

Sasha, from Stalin to Obama, A Biography, Create Space 2016

Shahnoza – Super Spy, A Novel, Create Space, 2016

Target Oahu, A Novel, Create Space, 2017

Aerosol, A Novel, Create Space, 2017

The Health Center, A Novel, Create Space, 2017

The Conservator, A Biography, Create Space, 2017

The Evil Alliance, A Novel, Create Space, 2018

Tehran Revisited, A Novel, Archway Publishers, 2019

St. Barnabas, A Novel, Inspiring Voices, 2019

The Caravan, A Novel, Outskirts Press, 2019

Senator McPherson, A Novel, Inspiring Voices, 2019

Meetings in Moscow, A Novel, Outskirts Press, 2019

Madam President, A Novel, Outskirts Press, 2019

Kiwi Country, A Novel, Outskirts Press, 2020

Inside Iran, A Novel, Outskirts Press, 2020

Introduction

My name is Jeffry Wilkens. My friends call me Jeff and I hope you will too, by the time you've read my story. I turned 90 years a few months ago and that means I probably don't have a whole lot of time left; so, while I'm still able, I need to get going.

I'm a long-ago-retired photo-journalist, and I've been blessed with good-enough health to have been able to travel to many, many places on Planet Earth. I'm also an avid fly fisherman, and that passion has taken me to many places. As my story unfolds, you'll see many of pictures I've taken, just to prove I *really* was there!

One

Let's begin with New Zealand. In the 1980s I visited New Zealand four times, three with my wife an one without her. When I went by myself it was in July, dead winter in those places in the Southern Hemisphere. I'm an avid fly fisherman and it was the fly fishing that drew me to New Zealand. If you look at a map of New Zealand's North Island, you'll see, almost in the center, Lake Taupo. That lake is home to some of the largest trout to be found anywhere. They're something like our Pacific Rim steelhead trout. They live in a large body of water (Lake Taupo or the Pacific Ocean) where they feed on minnows and other small fish and when it's time for them to spawn, they move into rivers. The Lake Taupo fish have a number of rivers to choose from, and one of their favorites is the Tongariro River, which flows into Lake Taupo near the small city of Turangi.

During each of my visits to North Island I stayed at the Tongariro River motel and got to know the owners quite well, Joy and Sam Cartwright. In fact, the time I went by myself, Sam lent me his beat-up 1983 Citroen sedan to use and I was able to drive to many of the best fishing waters in New Zealand.

I remember fishing near the mouth of the Tongariro, in waist-deep water near Lake Taupo's shoreline. It was in July and the sun was quite low in the northern sky. On that memorable day I hooked and released three Brown trout, each in the three-to-five pound range. Here's a picture of me that a friend took.

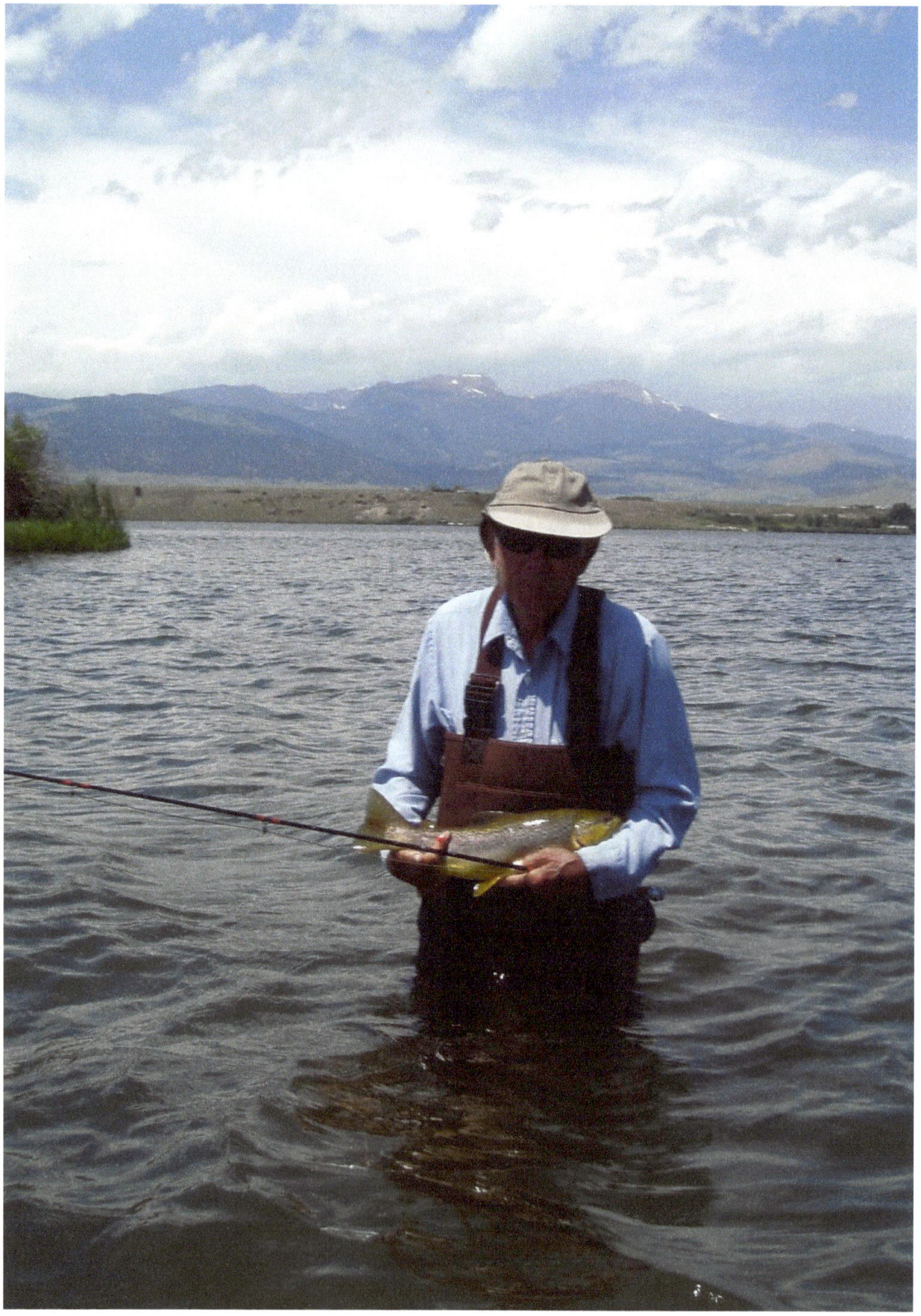

As you probably know, New Zealand is a two-island country. South Island is home to the so-called Southern Alps, a long string of snow-capped mountains that rise to some 10,000 feet about sea level, with the Tasman Sea just to the west. To the east, alongside the Pacific Ocean, is the city of Dunedin, settled many years ago by immigrants from Scotland. One of Dunedin's principal tourist attractions is the Royal Albatross colony which lies on a steep hillside a few miles north of the city. These magnificent birds have a wingspan of ten to twelve feet and they're capable of soaring along the ocean surface, for miles, without flapping their wings, using the wave-induced updrafts to sustain their flight. When I visited the viewing site I was able to get a picture of an adult about to feed its youngster.

Two

Now I'm going to write a few lines about Kamchatka. If you've never heard of that place, you're not alone. If you look at a map of the north Pacific Ocean, you'll see the Kamchatka peninsula pointing southward toward Japan. In landmass, it's about the same size as California. To understand my interest in this place I'll recall a brief bit of history.

During the Cold War, the Soviet leaders in the Kremlin made Kamchatka an off-limits territory to everyone except the native Koryaks who had lived there for ages, plus a few thousand Russians who were mostly located in the region's capital, Petropavlovsk-Kamchatsky.   The reason for this made sense, to the Soviets. The Soviet's Pacific Ocean nuclear submarine fleet's home was at Avacha Bay, a few kilometers west of Petropavlovsk and that, of course, was strictly off-limits to anyone who wasn't already cleared to work there.

The far-northern part of the peninsula was also off-limits because it was used as an impact zone for the Soviet's testing of their Intercontinental Ballistic Missile program.

Why is this important? Because with these restrictions in place for twenty or so years, the peninsula was petty much the way Mother Nature made it: almost no human impact on the peninsula's environment.

Now we get to the good part. Kamchatka is home to any number of rivers, rivers that flow westward into the Sea of Okhotsk, and to the east into the Pacific Ocean. Because the peninsula lies at about the same latitude as Alaska, those rivers are clear and cold, much like the rivers in the Pacific Northwest: Oregon, Washington state and British Columbia. As such, they are home to all five sub-species of salmon and, especially, to the steelhead trout.

It is the steelhead trout, *Oncorhynchus mykiss,* or, simply, the steelhead, that I want to write about.

***

In the mid-1990s, a group of dedicated conservationists, clustered mostly in the Seattle area, decided to partner with the Russian government and send an expedition to Kamchatka, there to study the steelhead trout that populated most of Kamchatka's easterly-flowing rivers. They knew that if they could study the life histories of these fish, they could compare them with the similar steelhead in the rivers of the Pacific Northwest. Those Northwest steelhead, most of them, were on the EPA's threatened or endangered lists, some populations on the verge of extinction. Whereas, the Kamchatka populations were pretty much as they had been from the beginning of time.

It was probably in October of 1997 that the first group of Americans gathered in Petropavlovsk and met their Russian counterparts, a small team of scientists from the Ichthyology Department of Moscow State University.

The Americans were fly fishermen, six of them, and their mission was simple. Catch and release unharmed as many steelhead as possible but before letting the fish return to the river, collect samples for eventual examination in a laboratory: a few scales (to determine the fish's age), its measurements (length and girth) and a ventral fin to examine later for DNA analysis. Some of these fish were tagged with a unique number so that if captured again, examination would reveal the location of the capture and how long since the original capture. This was important because most steelhead in the Pacific Northwest return to their natal rivers no more than once, rarely twice, before they die. To the astonishment of the researchers, one Kamchatka steelhead was captured on its *eleventh* visit to its natal stream. This one example helps explain why the Kamchatka populations are so vast. Every time the fish returns, he/she increases the population, so the numbers expand exponentially.

*　*　*

Being the newshound that I am, the expedition allowed me join it for a few days and I got some pictures that are probably unique. The expedition had set up a camp alongside the Kvachina River, known to hold a number of large steelhead trout. As I said, it was October and the fall colors were in full display. This photo show a fly fisherman—I was unable to get his name—patiently waiting for a steelhead to grab his fly.

* * *

This close-up photo shows a fisherman collecting a sample of scales. In another moment or two, he'll release the fish—unharmed—back into the river.

This next photo is one of my favorites. It shows the Kamchatka *tundra* with a fisherman slowly making his way back to camp. Tundra is spongy, uneven and wet; and very difficult to walk on. But the picture gives you some idea of how vast and empty is this part of Kamchatka.

This last image tells us why people love to fish for Kamchatka steelhead. These are BIG fish.

The expedition was prepared for a truly wilderness experience. No electricity, no running water, no convenient toilet facilities The tents in which the party ate, slept and changed clothes, were a bright orange, why I never learned. If you look closely, you'll see an American and a Russian flag, showing that this was a truly international, cooperative expedition.

One might ask, how does one travel in a region without roads? In Kamchatka they do it by flying in the MI-8 helicopter, a holdover from the bad old days of Soviet rule. The MI-8 is arguably the most reliable and long-serving aircraft of its kind. Here's what one looks like.

And, finally, one last photo of something that is unique to Kamchatka, the Steller's Sea Eagle, the world's largest of the eagle species. It was first seen and named by Georg Steller, the German naturalist who accompanied Vitus Bering on his ill-fated voyage to discover Alaska, this in 1740. I did not take this picture, one of the expedition members did; but as the Steller's Sea Eagle—other than in Kamchatka—can now be found only in zoos, I thought it was worth keeping.

Steller's Sea Eagle

Three

Now I'm going to shift gears and write about my experiences in Iran. All of this happened a long time ago, long before computers and iPhones. I was just beginning my life as a photo-journalist and a friend of mine, who was working at the American embassy in Tehran, invited me to come and stay with him for as long as necessary. Sammy Kincaid was still single but he had a two-bedroom apartment on Ferdowsi Avenue, not far from the embassy compound. And, he was the junior officer in the embassy's three-man consular office, so it was easy enough for him to apply for an entry visa, in my name.

This was, mind you, while shah Mohammad Reza Pahlavi was still in power, some years before he was run out of Iran by Ayatollah Khomeini in 1979.

Here's a map to remind us what we're talking about. (You can see how close Sanandaj is to the Iraqi frontier. More of this below.)

Well, no more than a week after I arrived in Tehran, Sammy tells me he wants to take me hunting. As we're both in our early thirties, he figures we're in good enough shape to climb into the mountains and hunt for *Ibex,* the species of mountain goat that prefers rocky ledges and inaccessible terrain. One of the embassy's local employees is a guy known to me only as 'Pop.' Pop is an Assyrian Christian who speaks Farsi (Persian) and pretty good English. And he's done this before, claims to know the mountains like the back of his hand.

So, we pile into Sammy's Land Rover and head west. We overnight in the small western city of Sanandaj—less that 50 miles from the Iraqi border—and Pop tells us we're now in Kurdish country. But before we left, early in the morning, I took this group picture.

Hunting party, Sanandaj. SK on Right.

It's faded red after all these years but you can see the Land Rover on the right. Pop is the third guy, right to left, Sammy is on Pop's right. The others are a few Kurdish youngsters who wanted to be in the picture.

Pop doesn't speak Kurdish but the next morning he finds a twenty-something guy who speaks both Farsi and Kurdish; and he'll be our guide. We drive the Rover westward to the end of the road and from there begin hiking uphill, up and up until I figure we're at least two thousand feet above the valley floor. Pop asks us to stop for a breather and while he's doing that I use my binoculars to scan the area. Sammy borrowed my camera and took this picture.

Ibex Country, near Iraqi border

* * *

Although there are a lot of mountains in Iran, there are some interesting places that are semi-tropical. One of these is accessible by auto and here's a photo of the countryside as one drives toward the Caspian Sea. If you look carefully, you can see that the locals are keeping their cattle's forage off the ground, on stilts. That's because it rains so much, much like western Washington and Oregon.

Semitropical Iran, near Caspian Sea

* * *

Back to the Land Rover. It's a go-anywhere four-wheel drive vehicle and I well recall a trip that Sammy made, with me as his passenger, high up in the Elburz Mountains at the top of a mountain pass.

Mountain Pass thru Elburz Mountains

That cliff-side road is all gravel with just enough space for two vehicles to meet, safely. Remember, this was many years ago. Today, the Persians probably have a four-lane, paved highway, through this same valley. But the photo shows the extent of the mountains, reaching nearly to the clouds above.

I have another photo that shows some interesting features; a deep river valley through the mountains, with a few adobe buildings clinging to the steep slope, and a two-way dirt road the follows the river downstream.

View from road to Caspian, the 'wet side' of Iran

* * *

Camel Caravan, Elburz Mountains

I took this photo while I was driving my Land Rover back to Tehran. I'd never seen camels before, not in Iran, and certainly not in the Elburz Mountain range. You can just make out the guy who's leading the four animals, one of which appears to be too young to carry a load.

* * *

Now I want to show you probably the most interesting photo in the whole collection. Those of you readers who are Christians, surely know the story of Noah's Ark and how it is supposed to have come to rest on the flanks of Mt. Ararat. (See Genesis, chapter seven.)

Well, a month of so after my arrival in Tehran, my friend Sammy asked me if I'd like to go on a *real* adventure. So I said Sure, why not? He told me he'd never done this before but he wanted to get as close to the Soviet Union's border with Iran as possible. At than point, it also intersects with the Turkish frontier.

So, we hop into his trusty Land Rover and off we go, heading almost due north. It takes us two days to get there but, eventually, we stop and I take this picture. You can see that there's a one wire telephone or telegraph wire and the road is unpaved. It's probably one of least-used roads in all of Iran.

Incidentally, this is the same road that was used by billionaire oil tycoon Ross Perot's team as he arranged to spring three of his EDS workers from a Tehran prison and bring them to safety at the Turkish border. You can read about it in Ken Follet's book, *On Wings of Eagles*.

Mt. Ararat, about 15 miles from the Iran Turkey USSR border intersection

* * *

You readers have probably heard of Beluga Caviar, the world's finest. Well, it used to be the world's finest because it came from Iran's Caspian Sea. Not anymore.

Overfishing and the international sanctions imposed on the mullahs have all but ended Iran's caviar industry.

But in those days, when Iran was still open to Western travelers and Western ideas, Beluga Caviar was one of its most profitable export commodities.

Here's how it works. The Beluga sturgeon, which have the same life expectancy, roughly, as humans, thrive in the shallow waters of the Caspian Sea's southern shoreline. In water no more than 15 feet deep, the water (which is slightly less salty than the oceans) supports many small fish and a thick reed growth. The fish have plenty of cover and food. The fishers work in teams because their nets are large and heavy. Here's a very old photo of one of those teams. You can see how shallow the water is, these men are probably about to move into somewhat deeper water.

Sturgeon Fishermen w/ nets, at Chalus

Today, Baluga Caviar comes from Russia and the city of Astrakhan, at the northern end of the Caspian Sea, in the shallow waters of the Volga River's mouth. There, the environment is much the same as it is in Iran's water's pictured above.

One more note. At the time this photo was taken, one kilogram (2.2 pounds) of Beluga Caviar sold for about 100 rials, or about $1.25. In Tehran, the black market guys would sell it for half that.

The average price today: $1.30 per ounce, IF one can find it.

Four

Next, we're going to write about Yellowstone National Park. The scenery is spectacular and I hope these photographs will do it justice.

The most popular feature of the park is its Grand Canyon. Every year thousands of visitors stop to see it.

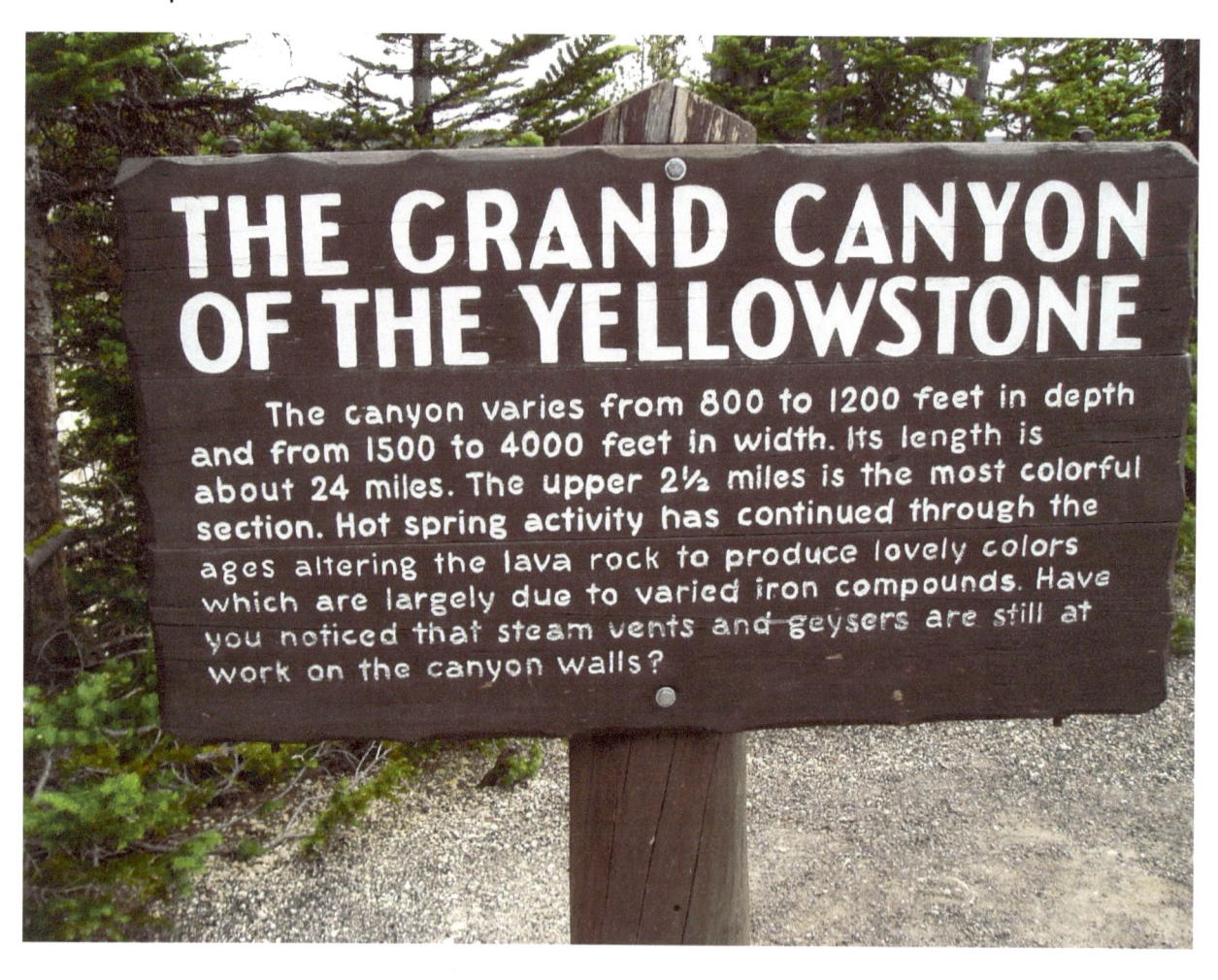

THE GRAND CANYON OF THE YELLOWSTONE

The canyon varies from 800 to 1200 feet in depth and from 1500 to 4000 feet in width. Its length is about 24 miles. The upper 2½ miles is the most colorful section. Hot spring activity has continued through the ages altering the lava rock to produce lovely colors which are largely due to varied iron compounds. Have you noticed that steam vents and geysers are still at work on the canyon walls?

Here's what the canyon looks like from one of the park's favorite viewpoints.

Several miles upstream of those falls, is a place to pull over and photograph the river.

This photo gives one an idea about what a huge, verdant meadow looks like.

Visitors are warned by signs and brief car-radio announcements NOT to feed the bears. Although there are occasional sightings of grizzly bears, most of them are black bears. It's not easy to photograph these creatures in full, but sometimes you get lucky and get a 'partial.' You can see that this bear has plenty to eat and they love to forage in lush, green grass.

The park's animals are free to go where they wish and there are breeding populations of some species. Here we see a doe attending to her very young fawn.

The National Park Service has a policy that requests its parks to 'respect nature.' In other words, no unnecessary interference. That means if a fire breaks out, let it burn so long as it's not threatening people or property. This photo shows an example of how that policy works.

There are a number of visitors' centers in the park, and some of them can be viewed from a distance. This center is dwarfed by its natural surroundings.

Here's a photo of the Yellowstone River which flows out of Yellowstone Lake, moving north. It becomes much larger as several tributaries flow into it farther north.

The visitor must keep his/her eyes open to see the all of the park's several wildlife species. Here is a photograph of a Prong Horned Antelope.

The park's animals, many of them, are accustomed to the crowds of tourists that come by every year. Here we see a mother elk with several of her offspring, enjoying the lush green grass which is free for the taking.

Here's another view of the Grand Canyon of the Yellowstone River. The canyon's walls have been worn away for eons, leaving some remarkable coloration.

From the highway pass that crosses the Continental Divide we see a pond covered with Lilly Pads. If you look carefully you can see two visitors, wearing shorts.

Believe it or not, even *Pelicans* stop over to rest, on their way to wherever they're going. Here's one near the opposite shore of the Yellowstone River.

It might be fair to say that Yellowstone Lake is the park's most spectacular attraction. It is the source of the Yellowstone River and is the largest body of fresh water in the park. See for yourself. Those snow-capped mountains and their runoff provide a constant source of water.

It could be said that the park's most notable feature is the Old Faithful geyser. For as long as anyone knows, the geyser 'lets go' about every sixty minutes, hence the name, Old Faithful. Here's just one photo of what it looks like.

One of the more popular tourist attractions in the park are its many 'mud pots.' These are formed, over hundreds of years, by the very slow upwelling of sulfurous mud and rock. And they smell like sulfur, or an old-fashioned outhouse. Even so, the tourists don't seem to mind. Notice the raised boardwalk at the bottom of the photo; apparently wet after a recent rain.

* * *

Well, those are some photographs of one of America's real treasures. Now, we'll move on to something else.

Five

As I said, I'm a photo-journalist. I mostly work for myself, selling stories and pictures to anyone who will buy them. But a few years ago, I wanted to build up a collection of photographs that I could use to impress a potential buyer, say a magazine, or newspaper, or even a television network. And so I decided to pay for—with my own money—a trip to China. As we all know, China is now America's chief competitor in the world of finance and commerce.

I went to the Chinese consulate in Washington, DC and after I told them why I wanted to visit China, they were more than happy to give me a visitor's visa, good for 30 days. There's a very good company, Viking Cruises, that specializes in small ships made for traversing rivers. So I booked passage on the Viking Century Sky, a six-deck ship that plies the Yangtze River. The non-stop flight from San Francisco to Shanghai took about eleven hours, another hour from the airport to the hotel, the name of which I've forgotten, but it certainly was luxurious, as shown by this photo of the lobby.

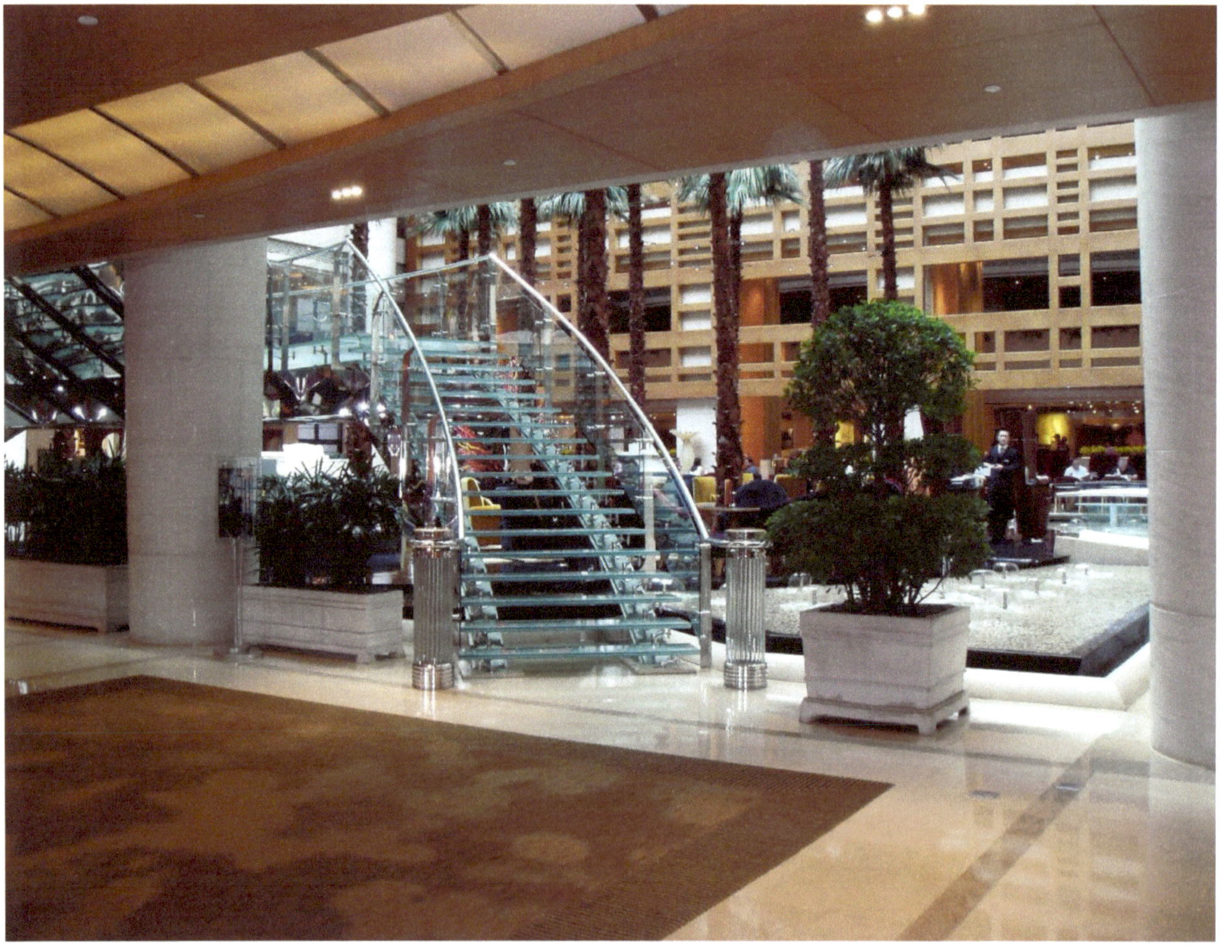

Our guide met my group at ten the next morning and after a brief ride in his convertible (a $50,000 Mercedes) this was what we saw at our first stop. Yes, those folks are all tourists, just like I am.

We took a water taxi to get some pictures of Shanghai from a distance. It's an impressive city, to be sure.

This four-deck ferry is mostly for Chinese passengers, as far as I could tell.

A lot of tourists, like me, used this broad sidewalk to enjoy a warm afternoon. Notice how many Western companies are advertising along this waterfront.

Part of the tour included a bus ride through a typical residential area. I thought it looked a bit shabby.

Shanghai is a coastal city, but its several canals have bridges to accommodate pedestrian traffic. Here, we see two covered bridges, spanning one of the canals.

This is a photo I took from a tour bus, the middle skyscraper is still being built. It is hard to see, but that object at the top of that tall spire is a red star, the symbol, in China, of its Communist heritage.

* * *

After two days in Shanghai, it was time to move on. Our Yangtze River trip began in the city of Wuhan and we boarded a Boeing 737 to get there.

* * *

Our group spent the night in Wuhan (I've forgotten the name of the hotel) and the next morning we boarded our Viking cruise ship, the *Century Sky*. It would be our home for the next week or so. Already, I could see that the river is dark and dirty.

Just before boarding our Century Sky, we could see how busy is this river-port city of Wuhan. Also, notice how smoggy the air seems to be. We'll see more of this later.

* * *

As part of its public relations program, Viking River Cruises supports a school for young children and, as such, our tour group spent most of a day visiting this facility. Our guide was a young Chinese fellow—nearly fluent in American English—who called himself *Max,* just to make it easy for us to remember. These photos are pretty much self-explanatory. Where they may not be, I'll provide a comment.

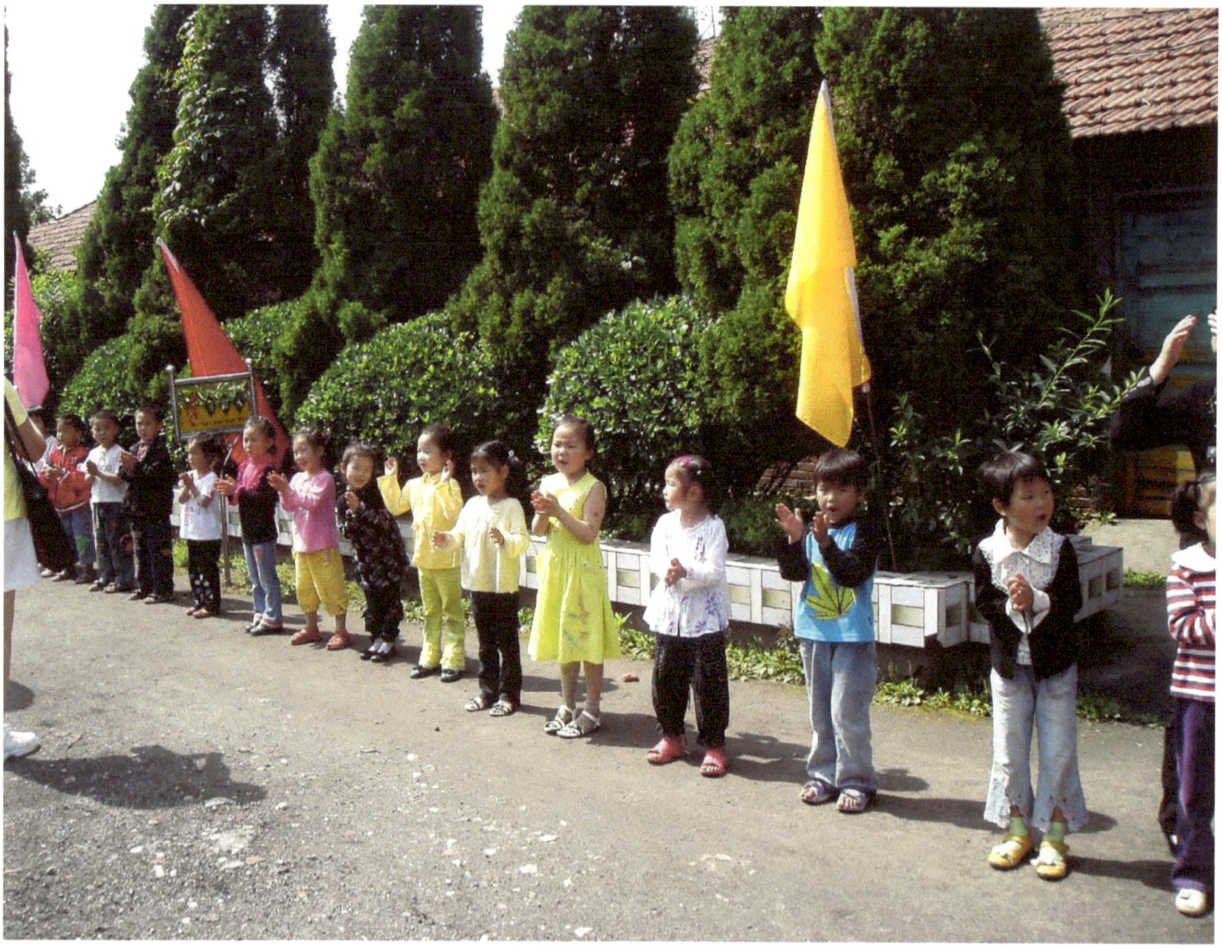

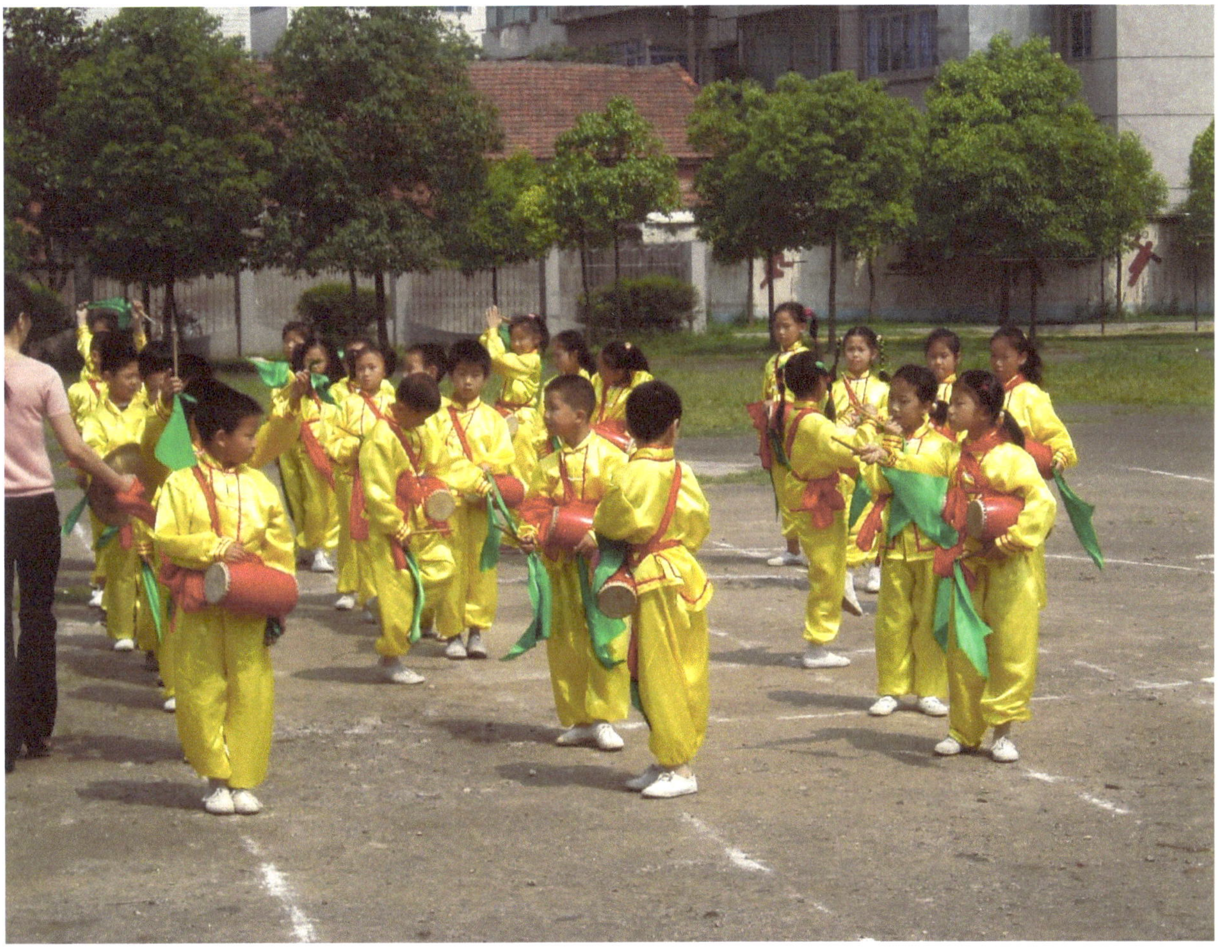

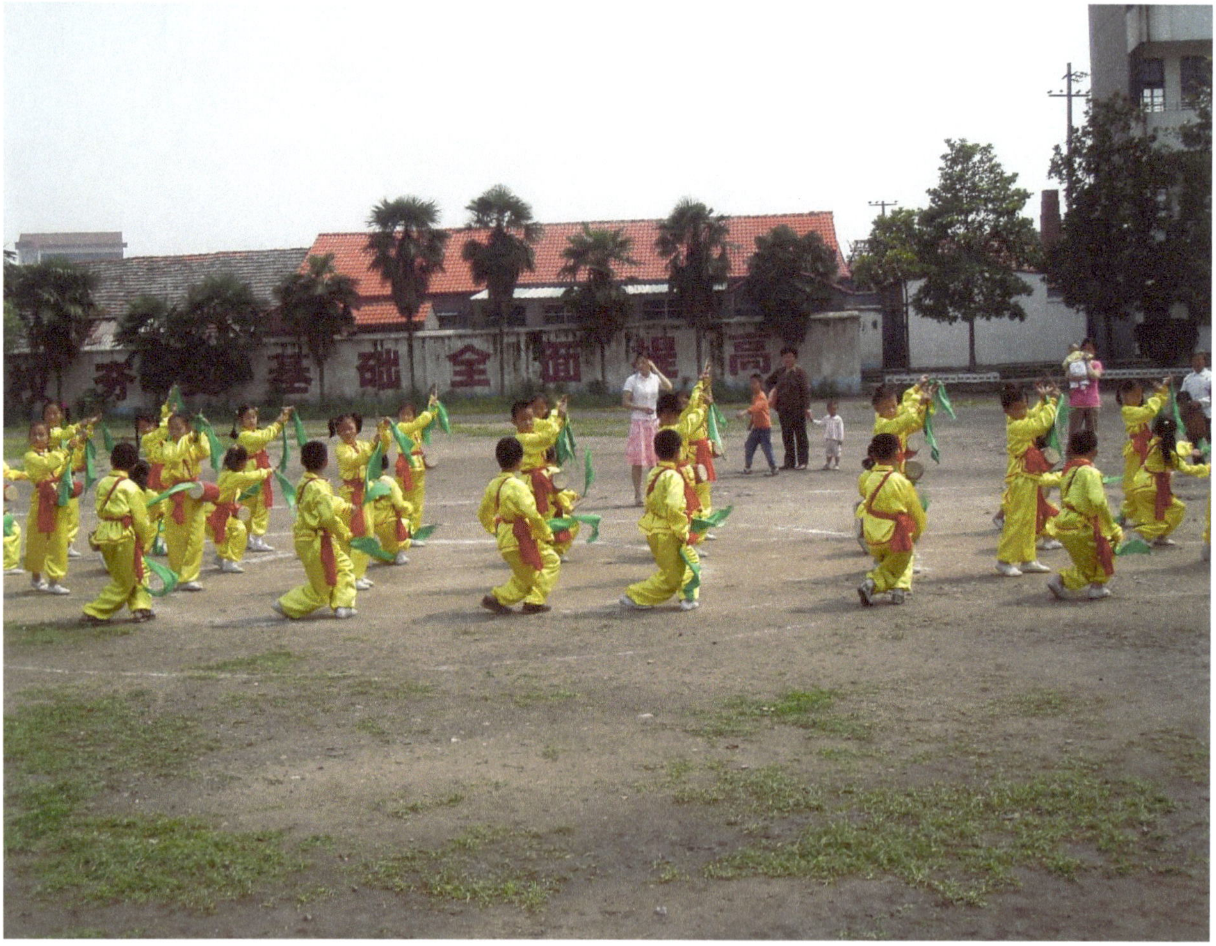
基础全面提高

This is our guide, Max, explaining to this classroom who we are and why we're here.

Here are three young girls, smiling their appreciation for our visit.

* * *

Time to move on. It's a huge river and there's much more to see.

This is the first of many cargo vessels that we'll see as we move upstream. This one is rather small and whatever it's carrying is covered.

Three cargo vessels just ahead of us. The air pollution is getting worse.

Who's to say what these ships are carrying, all of it important to the Chinese economy.

* * *

This Viking River Cruise's major attraction was the ship's passage through and alongside construction of the Three Gorges Dam, China's most ambitious construction project, to that time. When completed, the project would provide ship passage and hydroelectric power for millions of Chinese citizens. This photo is the first of many, as our ship enters one of the several locks that will be traversed as we move upstream.

The ship on the right is carrying nothing but automobiles, each of them made in China and, likely, most designed for export. Don't try to count them, it's impossible.

This photo gives us some idea of the enormity of the project. The blue earth mover in the foreground is probably no more than ten feet long. And, how much earth has been removed, on the right side of the photograph?

Another view, from our cruise ship.

Here we see a place where tourists, like me, can take pictures. Notice the blue vehicle on the right, for scale.

Here we see hydropower. Lots of it.

The Chinese authorities recognize the propaganda value in making our visit pleasant. Here we see park benches, our tour bus--comfortably at rest—while I, and a bunch of others, use the rest rooms and enjoy a pre-packaged lunch.

This photograph, taken from high above the project, shows the completed dam. Unfortunately, China's air pollution—the result of a zillion coal-fired stoves and furnaces—seriously impacts the view.

Below, the tour bus parking lot.

* * *

Part of the tour package includes a side trip, in a much smaller vessel, up the Jialing River. It flows through a narrow canyon and offers spectacular views. After an hour or so, we'll dock and have lunch at a restaurant that caters to Viking Cruise customers.

I had forgotten, but we began the cruise with a light rain falling.

I often ask myself when I see a structure like this one: How in the world can they do that?

One of those steep canyon walls. The tourists seem to be as awestruck as I was.

More of the same. If you look closely you'll see another boat just ahead of us.

Finally, we reach our destination. From the signage above, it's pretty obvious that Viking Cruises has a lot to do with this.

This is the view from inside the restaurant. You can see there are two ships. Ours is the one with the flying bridge.

* * *

Back on the Yangtze River, the two-man crew let me take this picture from inside the wheelhouse.

At the end of the cruise, we tourists have a long walk from the ship to the waiting busses that will take us back to our hotel. It will be nice to say goodbye to all that smog.

* * *

From Shanghai, our group flew to Xian, home to the so-called Terra Cotta Army, which, in my humble opinion, should rank as one of the seven or eight Wonders of the World. Here's what Wikipedia tells us about this.

"The Terracotta Army was discovered on March 29,1974 by farmers digging a water well approximately one mile east of the Qin Emperor's tomb, a region riddled with underground springs and watercourses. For centuries, occasional reports mentioned pieces of terracotta figures and fragments of the Qin burial site—roofing tiles, bricks and chunks of masonry. This discovery prompted Chinese archaeologists, to investigate, revealing the largest pottery figurine group ever found. A museum complex has since been constructed over the area, the largest pit being enclosed by a roofed structure."

I'll add my few words. Every individual soldier is different and if one looks closely at the faces, that becomes evident. They are life-size. Part of the lore says that Emperor Qin, who died at a very young age, wanted to be surrounded by soldiers, for his eternal protection.

I'll show a few of the photos I took, no need for comment, they speak for themselves.

74

This broad pavilion is the starting point for visiting the Great Wall of China. As I recall there was a reasonable admission price, but it was well worth whatever it cost. Just a few photos and then we'll leave China and move on to something else, the Free State of Ireland.

Tourists gathering to begin their walk up and along the wall.

Although it's not easy to see, the wall extends to the top of that hill and for miles and miles beyond.

Six

A few years ago, a friend of mine and I were having a beer in the local tavern. I was complaining that after China any other place I went would be a hard act to follow. No way, he said. You absolutely *must* see Ireland; some of the most fantastic scenery anywhere.

I figured that was a bit of hyperbole but I decided to give it a try. I was not disappointed, as I hope you'll agree.

To make things simple, I decided to go with a tour group, this one calls itself Globus. I suppose that suggests that it uses buses to go anywhere on the globe.

As I recall, my group flew into Ireland's capital city, Dublin, and we began the tour there. It might help if I show a map of Ireland, to remind us where we are.

Here's a photo of the hotel where I stayed, a nice place and not too expensive, calls itself the New Shamrock.

Behind the hotel was this well-kept garden, with a few guests enjoying themselves.

As everybody should know, Ireland is mostly Catholic and there are shrines everywhere that remind the tourist of this. I took this phot from my tour bus seat. Unfortunately, there's a bit of glare, which I should have foreseen.

This next photo shows one of those beautiful seascapes that I'd heard so much about.

Here's another one, taken about a half-hour later.

This could be dangerous if one were to stray off the approved walkways. The sign says so.

This photo, taken from my tour bus, gives you an idea of what typical Irish countryside looks like. Pretty hard to improve on.

Another favorite among us tourists. A very old castle on the far side of a small river. I should have asked if the place is occupied!

Although it was only about eleven o'clock, the tour bus driver wanted us to see what a real Irish pub looks like. Notice it's featuring Guinness, as in the world-famous Guinness ale.

More countryside, with very few people.

No, this is not a bomb shelter. It's a very old tomb and there are quite a few of them in this part of Ireland.

Our guide told us that this rock bears an inscription put there, probably, a thousand years ago. If he told us what it means, I've forgotten.

This beautiful park is just a few blocks from the center of downtown Dublin.

The tour bus driver told us we were moving through one of the more affluent neighborhoods in Dublin and stopped so we could photograph this entryway. From the plaque, it appears to be an apartment building. One wonders how those lovely vines are tended.

One of many Catholic churches in Dublin. Judging from its size, it has to be well-supported by its congregation.

As in England, traffic moves in the *left* lane. Our driver joked that this particular tunnel is his biggest challenge.

My notebook reminds that it was quite windy, with rain threatening, when I took this picture.

This is Blarney Castle, built sometime in the 11th century. It is Ireland's favorite tourist destination, but only for those who intend to kiss the Blarney Stone. Here's what Wikipedia says about that.

"At the top of the castle lies the Stone of Eloquence, better known as the Blarney Stone. Tourists visiting Blarney Castle may hang upside-down over a sheer drop to kiss the stone, which is said to give the gift of eloquence. There are many versions of the origin of the stone, including a claim that it was the Lia Fáil — a numinous stone upon which Irish kings were crowned."

Believe it or not, I climbed to the top of the tower and there was guy there who charged two dollars to hold my legs while I leaned way out to kiss the stone. Was it worth it. Of course!

* * *

Somewhere in my youth I remember hearing the phrase 'That's all she wrote,' probably referring to a letter written to a soldier during one of America's wars. I'm going to mimic that phrase by saying this is all I'm going to write, about Ireland.

Next, we'll take a look at South America.

Seven

I saved enough money to book passage on one of Holland America's most luxurious cruise ships, the S.S. Rotterdam, named after the seaport city of the same name in Holland. The itinerary really appealed to me because I'd be visiting parts of the world I'd never seen before. My group was to fly from San Diego to Santiago, Chile, spend two days there, then take a tour bus down to Valparaiso, Chile's only deep water sea port. We'd board the Rotterdam there and then sail south to Cape Horn, then turn north and end at Rio de Janeiro, the former capital of Brazil.

One could say that the SS Rotterdam is *posh* ship, meaning fancy, nice, luxurious, whatever. What many people don't understand is where that word, posh, came from. In the 18th-19th centuries, British sailing ships traveled back and forth from England to India, to assure the Empire of an adequate supply of Indian tea. Posh = **P**ort **O**ut, **S**tarboard **H**ome. That is, those passengers who could afford it booked space on the left (port) side of the vessel while sailing toward India, and on the right (starboard) side coming home. Why? To avoid the blistering sun. Makes sense, doesn't it?

* * *

Here's a photo of our ship about an hour before it left its pier at Valparaiso. You can see how its size compares with the people and vehicles, lower left.

Shortly after we arrived in Santiago, our tour bus stopped so we passengers could photograph a scene showing the Chilean flag, several of them.

Our bus driver let us out long enough to photograph the façade of Chile's capital building.

Downtown Santiago. Nobody's perfect and the man in the foreground doesn't know how badly I goofed!

* * *

Santiago lies at the bottom of a broad valley and a few of us tourists got out of the bus to take this picture. It appears to be large and crowded.

Somewhere along the route, our driver stopped so we could photograph a typical farmers' market. When I took this picture I failed to notice the youngster pushing his toy truck.

Another farmers' market photograph.

* * *

One of the advertised treats was a bus ride up to the Continental Divide, maybe a two hour trip. On the way back, I was disappointed to see this scene: a kind of mud flat with a smaller cruise ship on the left. It might even be grounded.

Eventually, we had to say goodbye to Santiago and took the long, down-hill bus ride to our waiting ship in the Valparaiso harbor.

* * *

The next morning our ship resumed her voyage, heading for the 'bottom of the world,' the Straits of Magellan and Cape Horn.

At first, we ran into a light rain, enough to keep most of us inside. But the skyline is threatening.

As our ship moves southward, the weather changes and it's cold now, as a glacier suddenly appears.

Finally, we reach the turning point, passing through the Magellan Strait and Cape Horn. This piece of water is known for howling winds and ferocious tides, enough to make passengers seasick. But not this time.

Looking due north, from the 'bottom of the world.'

Another day, and our ship arrives in Sao Paulo. We'll spend a day here before moving on to Rio.

Downtown Sao Paulo. Then men are in shirt sleeves so it's a warm day.

Next stop, one of the city's better-known pieces of modern sculpture.

* * *

It takes our ship most of one day to move from Sao Paulo to Rio de Janeiro, the last stop on our cruise. The *must-see* attraction in Rio is the statue of Christ, purchased high on a the side of steep hill. The view from up there is spectacular, as you will see.

The statue is so large it's hard to get a decent photo but this was the best I could do.

Rio, from about one thousand feet above.

I took a taxi to my hotel. This broad boulevard skirts the ocean shoreline, on the left.

On of Rio's more popular beaches, as seen from my hotel room.

About nine in the morning. The tourists have yet to appear.

A three-sail sailboat, just on the horizon.

When these two youngsters saw me with my camera, they decided to show off.

* * *

That pretty much does it for my South American adventure. The next morning the tour operator's voucher paid for my taxi ride to Rio's airport. From their I took a Brazil Air Boeing 737 to Miami.

Eight

It shouldn't surprise anyone to learn that we photo-journalists are a kind of loosely-knit fraternity. We stay in touch with each other with emails, some of us use Face Book, others prefer Skype. It was about two months ago that I received an email from Jim Holbrook, a *Seattle Times* reporter/photographer. He invited me to come to his Emerald City, to have a look for myself.

All of this is happening on Elliot Bay, Seattle's salt-water playground.

* * *

Aboard our Argosy Cruiser. What you see there is Seattle's Great Wheel, in operation since late June of 2012. It's the largest Ferris Wheel on the West Coast and the gondolas at the top are 175 feet above the water. Each of the 42 gondolas is climate-controlled and can carry as many as eight passengers. When fully occupied there are more than 300 people enjoying the 12-minute, three revolution ride.

* * *

Here we see Seattle's iconic Space Needle, built for Seattle's 1962 World's Fair. The top of the structure is 605 feet above the surface. During the fair's opening week, more than two million visitors attended and each day about 20,000 people rode the elevators to the Needle's observation platform.

* * *

From our Argosy Cruiser I took this picture of the Victoria Clipper. The Clipper is the fastest passenger-carrying ship on the West Coast, cruising at about 35 mph, between Seattle and Victoria, British Columbia.

That's Beacon Hill, a long way off but there are at least three television transmission towers. It's the highest part of the city and that's why those towers are there.

This is the Pacific Northwest's principal grain storage and delivery facility, at Terminal 86. Three railroad companies (Burlington Northern, Santa Fe and Union Pacific) deliver grain—mostly from eastern Washington's grain-growing Palouse region—to the facility, where it is stored in those several towers. Then, a system of conveyor belts moves the grain into position where it can loaded onto ocean-going ships.

* * *

That's Alki Point, and the vast reaches of Puget Sound beyond.

* * *

As our Argosy Cruiser heads for home, we pass the mouth of the Duwamish Waterway, Seattle's principal maritime docking and ship-repair facility.

* * *

A closer view. This enormous container-cargo vessel is registered in Hamburg, Germany.

An interesting photograph. In the foreground is a United States Coastguard Cutter, identified by the diagonal red stripe on its starboard bow. Far beyond the cutter is the very top Century Link Field, home of the Seattle Seahawks. Farther right, the top of T-Mobile Park, home to the Seattle Mariners.

* * *

The end of our tour. We get a sense of the importance to Seattle's economy of all this dock-side activity.

Nine

At the beginning of this narrative I said that I'm an avid fly fisherman. I'd never fished in the Pacific Northwest until I got an invitation from a member of the Washington Fly Fishing Club, most of whose members live in the Seattle area. It told me that I should fly out to Seattle, then hire an Avis rental and meet him at a motel in Vantage. Vantage is a village located on the south side of the Columbia River, at the point where Interstate 90 crosses that river. He told me he would arrange to book two rooms and that we could take our meals from the small restaurant sited next to the motel.

Fortunately, my friend had all the necessary gear: fishing vests, two float tubes, two pairs of flippers and stocking-foot waders. Bring your own fly rod and flies, he told me.

* * *

By the time I got to the motel, 15 hours after leaving home, I was pretty well worn out. So Bill and I—that's his name, Bill Anderson—spent the night in our two separate rooms. The next morning we had breakfast together in the Riverside Restaurant.

"What's the deal here, Jeff? Where are we going and how do we get there?"

"Simple, Bill. I've already put our gear in you rental. We drive across the bridge—that's Interstate 90—turn right after crossing the river, then we find our way to the village of Beverly. I've been there many times, so we won't get lost. At Beverly, we take a left and drive along the Crab Creek road until we get to the Lenice Lake parking lot. From the lot we haul our stuff to water's edge, inflate our float tubes, crawl into our waders, slip on the flippers, and we're ready to go."

"Why Lenice Lake and not some other?"

"Because my club has its annual outing at Lenice. They're some very nice Rainbow trout in that lake, once in a while up to two pounds. The Wildlife Department keeps the lake stocked; it hauls a zillion fingerlings in a tank truck, sluices them through a long plastic tube into the lake and within a year of so, they're legal size."

"What's legal?"

"Eight inches, but you'll rarely hook one of those."

"Catch and release?"

"Actually, the regs allow you to keep one fish a day. But you wouldn't want to eat one. I've tried it, they taste muddy. So, yeah, it amounts to catch and release."

* * *

Bill and I fished parts of two days. Three hours in the morning and three in late afternoon. Here are the pictures I took along the way.

A convenient place to get into the lake; shallow and protected from the wind.

On the right is Bill, getting his fly rod out of its tube. He prefers that banana boat to a float tube. I'm on the left, fiddling with something.

Bill is on his way. He's wearing waders because his feet are actually in the water. He may also be wearing flippers, just in case.

I took this picture a few minutes before Bill got going, looking east. There's heavy reed growth there and that's because the lake is being fed by another body of water farther east. Those heavy reeds are home to various types of bird life. The very shy Bittern—about the size and shape of a stork—likes that kind of habitat because he's nearly invisible when standing motionless.

Bill moved across the lake rather quickly and that's because his banana boat has oars, like a rowboat. He may be seeking protection from the wind which, at times, blows so hard as to prevent fly fishing.

Each of these guys is fishing out of a float tube.

Here we see a pair of White Pelicans and they're not shy about being photographed.

Sometime later, the same pair taking flight.

One of the neat things about Lenice Lake. If you get close enough to the water's edge there are some beautiful desert flowers to photograph. The green foliage is typical desert sage brush.

More of the same. That ridge in the background is part of the Saddle Mountain chain. It's a favorite jumping-off spot for those daredevil para-glider people, because it provides about 1,500 vertical feet of unobstructed air space.

I was able to get close enough to this Redwing Blackbird to get his picture before he spooked.

Another Redwing, taking cover in a Russian Olive tree.

The lake attracts all kinds of waterfowl and those reeds along the shore provide the cover the small trout need if they're to survive the predations of the larger fish. The large tree is a Russian Olive, a hardy species that grows along the water's edge.

This picture amazes me every time I see it. This is a very large raccoon, seeking cover after it senses my presence. Now, we know that raccoons are fish eaters but, ask yourself, how does a raccoon capture fish in a lake like this one?

Ten

While we're hopscotching from one country to another, let's try something different. Our neighbor to the north has some interesting things to see and do. I recently visited Waterton Lakes National Park, in Alberta, Canada. It goes without saying that I took a few pictures. Let's have a look.

* * *

This is Waterton Village at the southern end of Waterton Lake. It's one of Canada's most popular tourist attractions. At an elevation of more than 4,000 feet, the park gets some snow in winter months, yet it is open year round.

Wildflowers are abundant, as this picture of Indian Paintbrush shows.

Bear Grass is another wildflower that grows only at the higher elevations.

Many families visit the park in motor homes. This one is equipped with satellite television. One wonders if anyone has ever scaled those peaks.

Sunset at dusk.

This two-year old White Tail doe is feeding on lush grass.

A good photographer never misses an opportunity like this one.

Waterton Mountain

Storm Clouds

We're going to leave Waterton Park and move to the southwest. More of that in the next chapter.

Eleven

My senior-citizen mom lives in one of those retirement communities, this one is right on the edge of Lake Washington in the small city of Mercer Island. It's kind of a pricey place to live, she tells me, but my dad, years ago, left her with a pretty healthy inheritance, enough that she can pay her bills without any help from me. When I visit her I always take my camera (surprise?) and I've collected a few photos to show what the grounds look like.

        I hope you like them.

        * * *

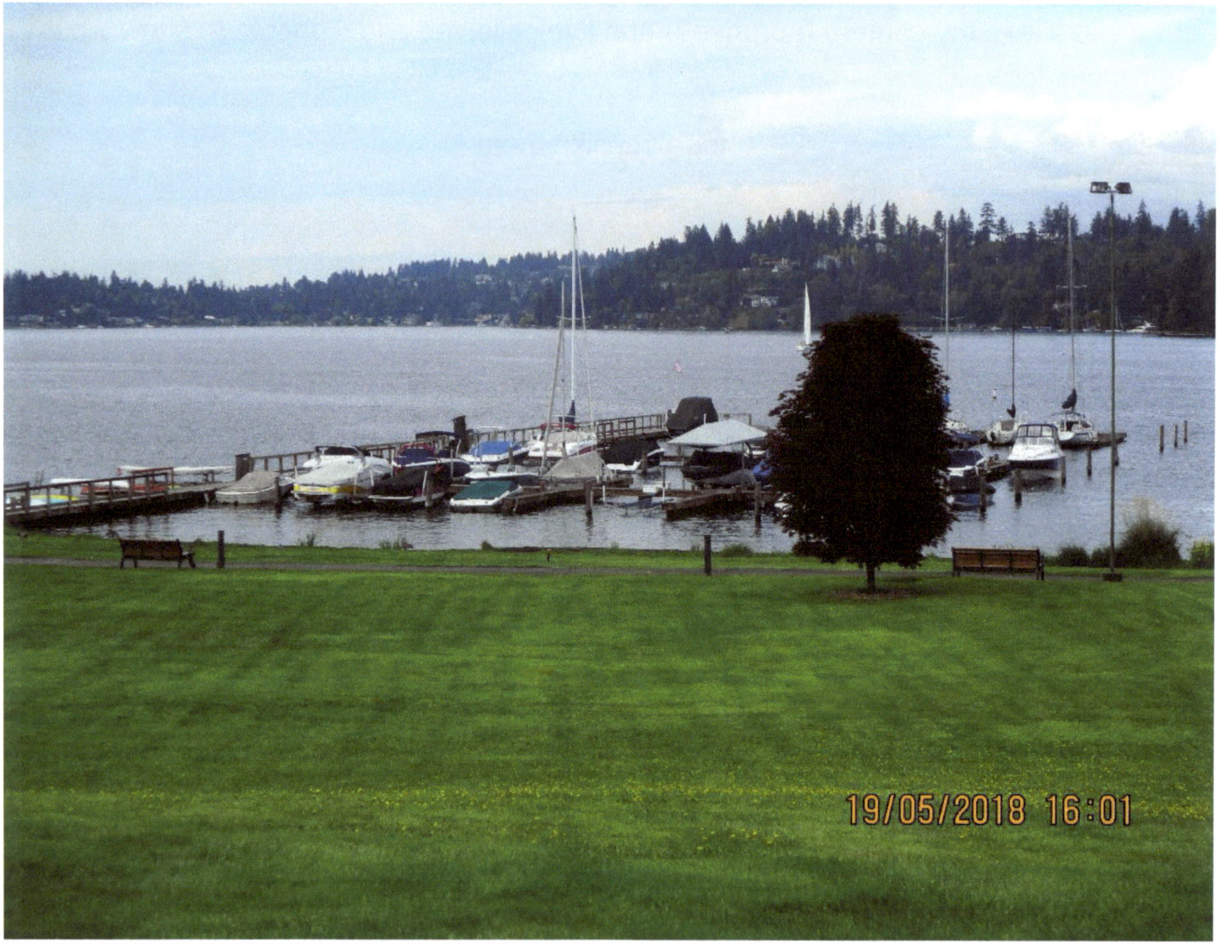
19/05/2018 16:01

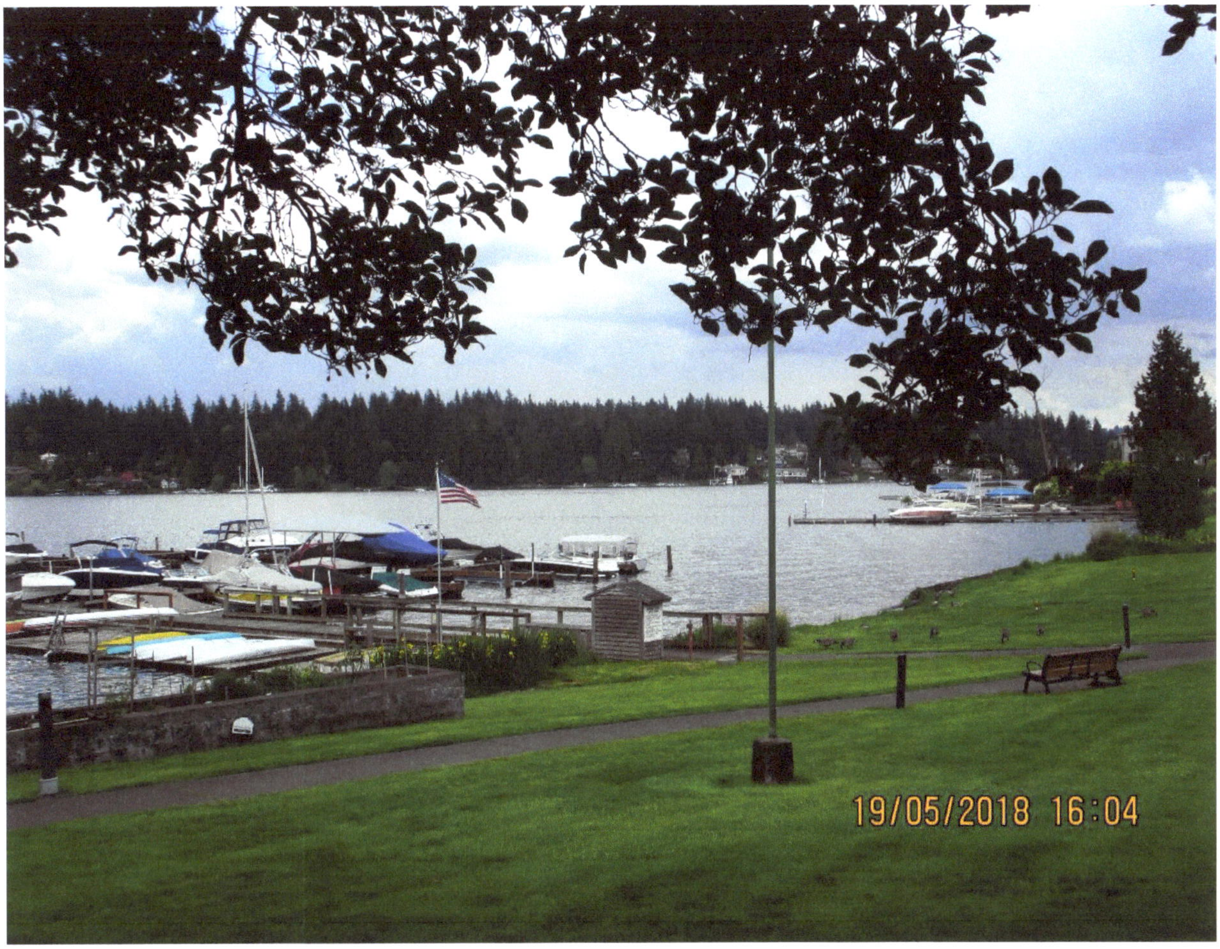
19/05/2018 16:04

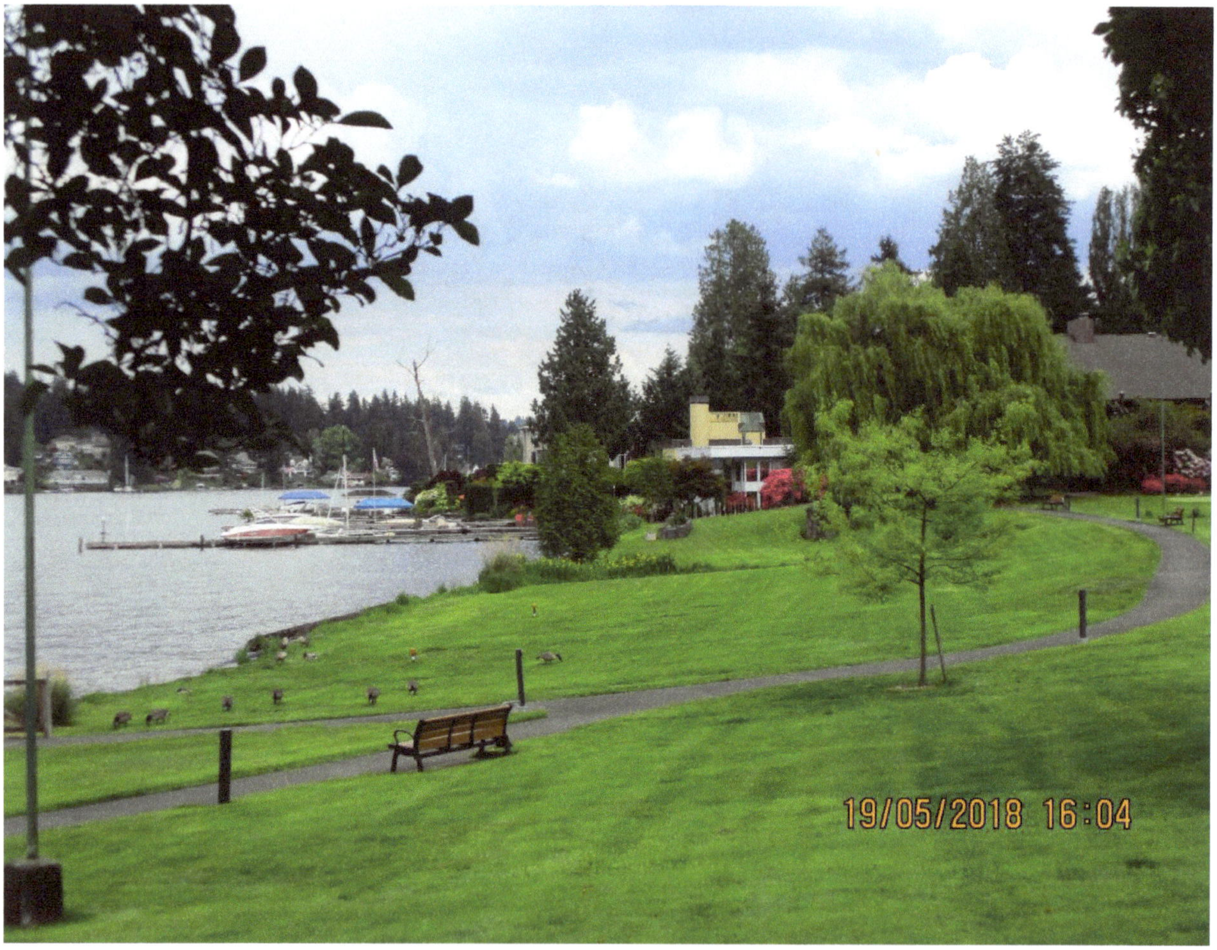
19/05/2018 16:04

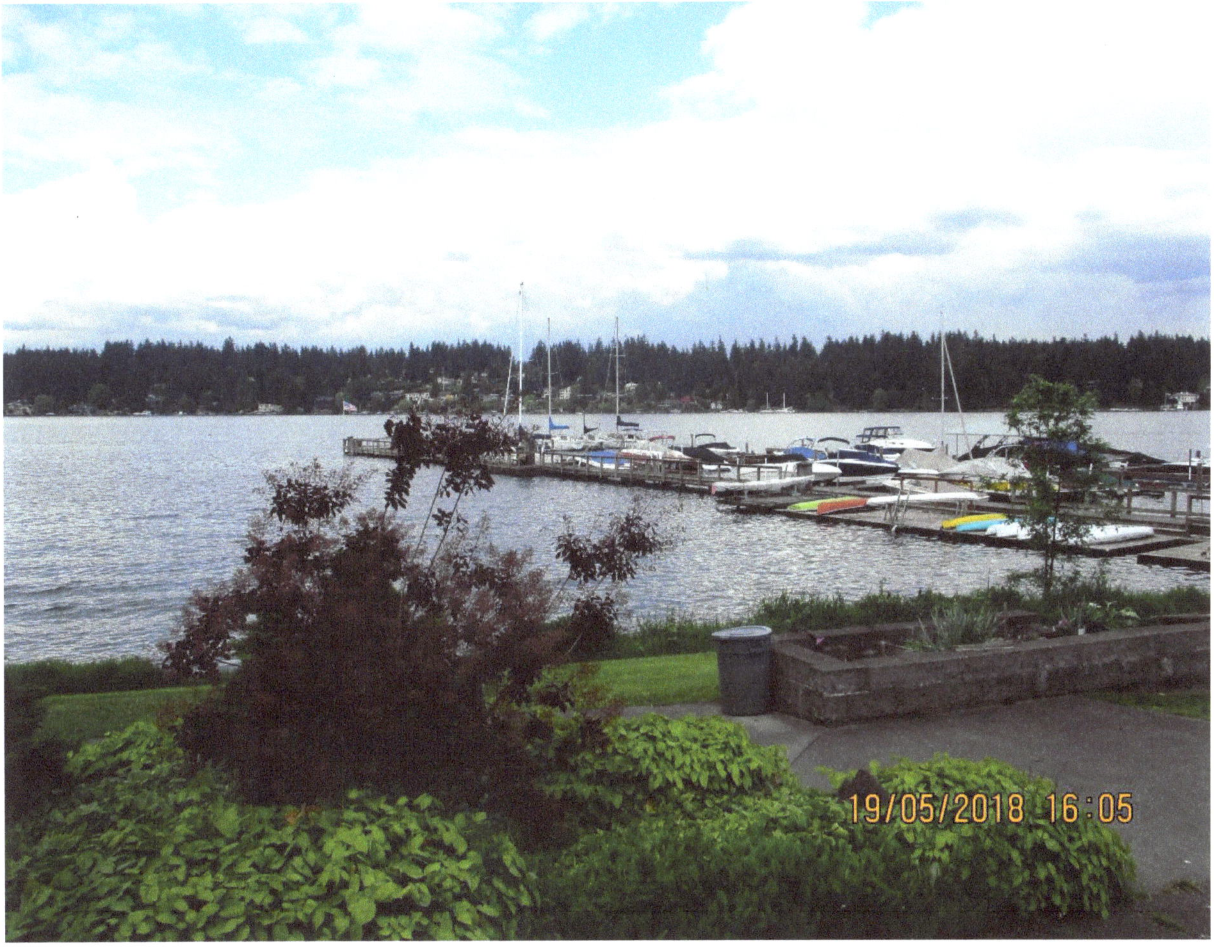
19/05/2018 16:05

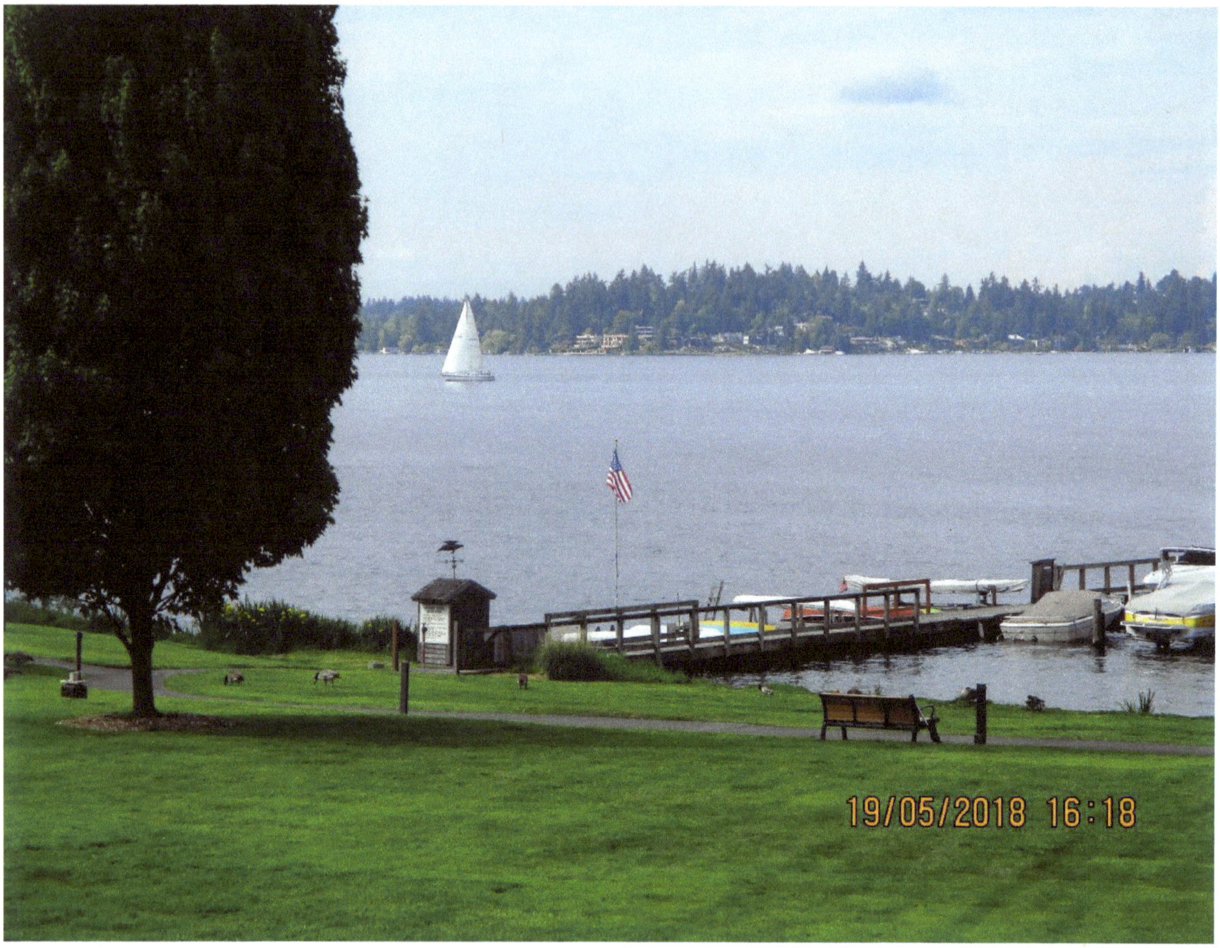
19/05/2018 16:18

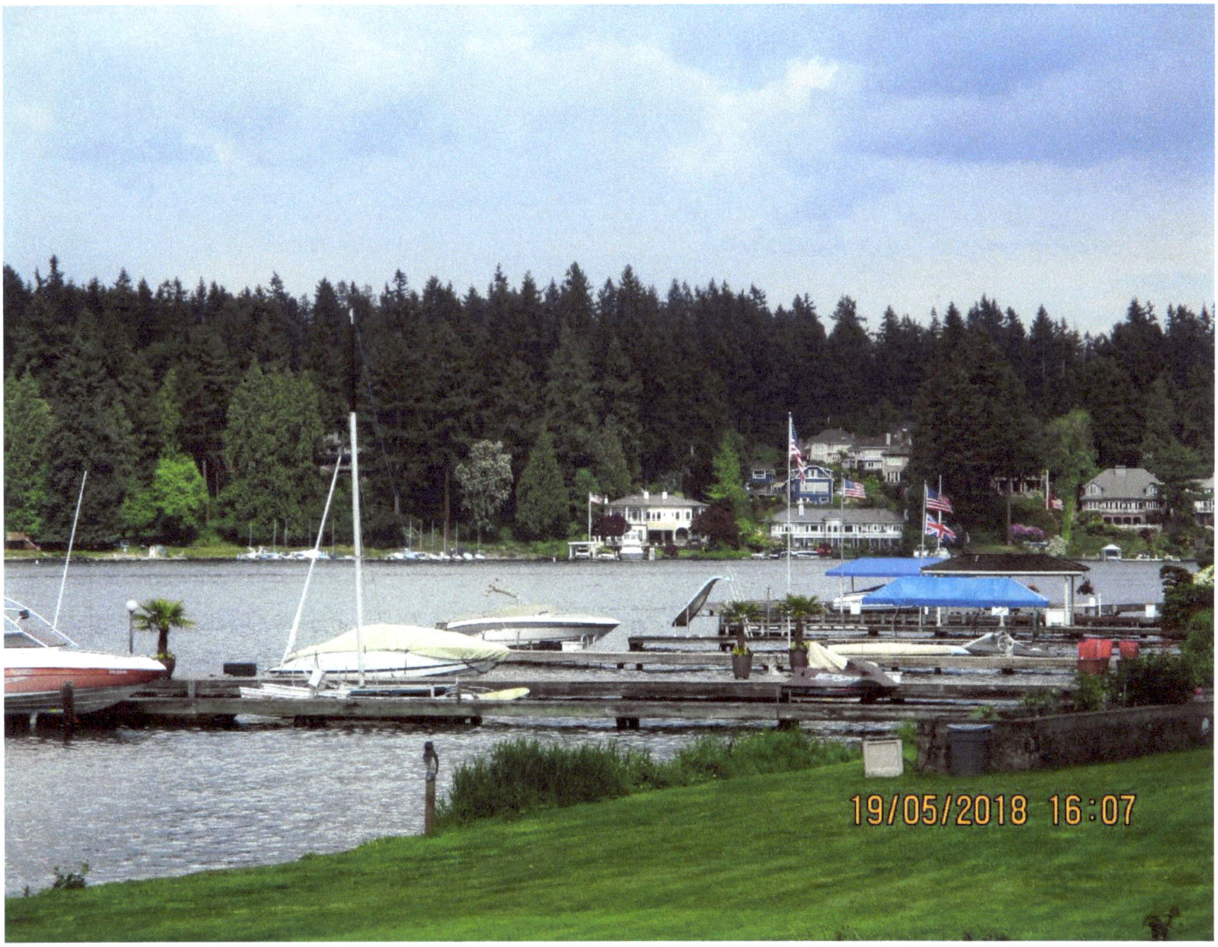
19/05/2018 16:07

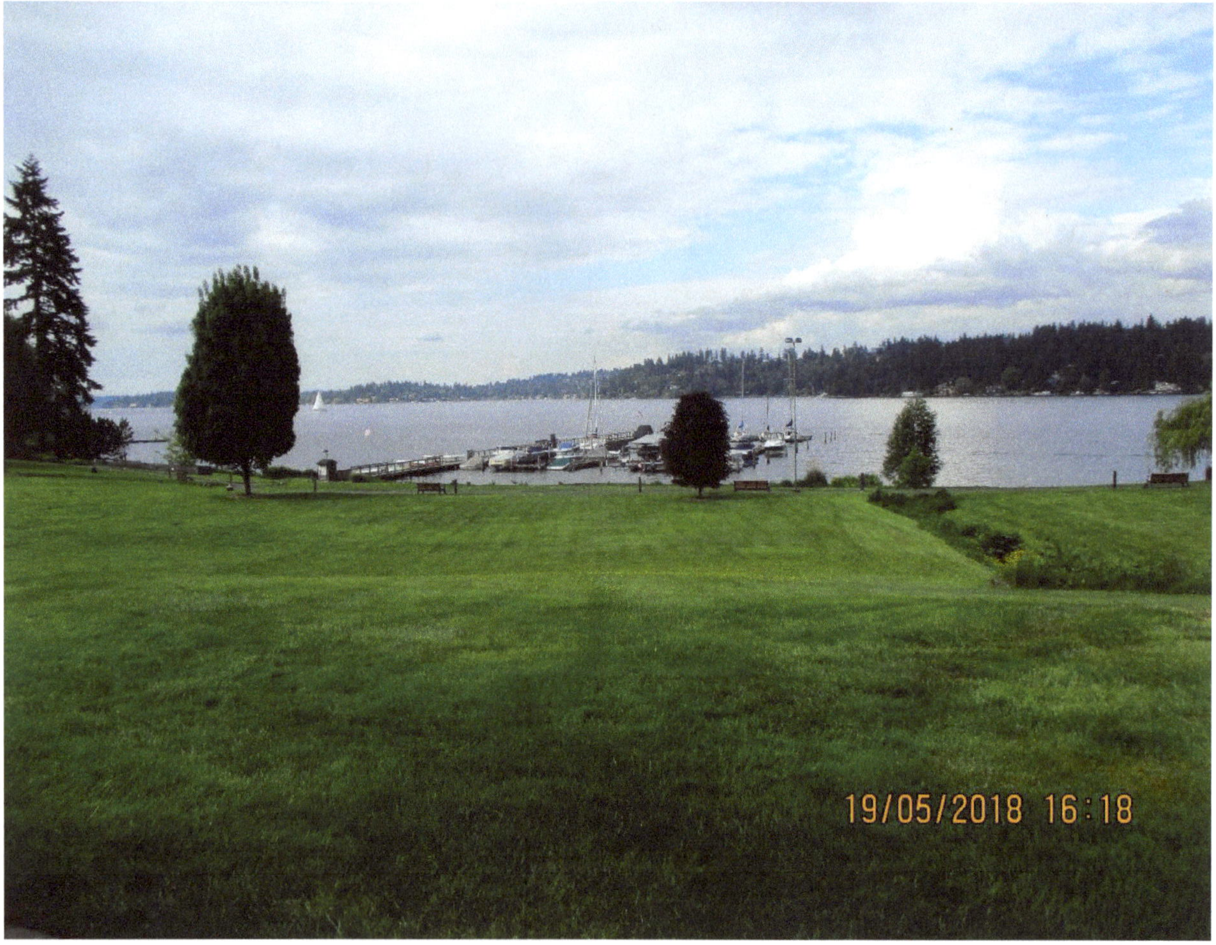
19/05/2018 16:18

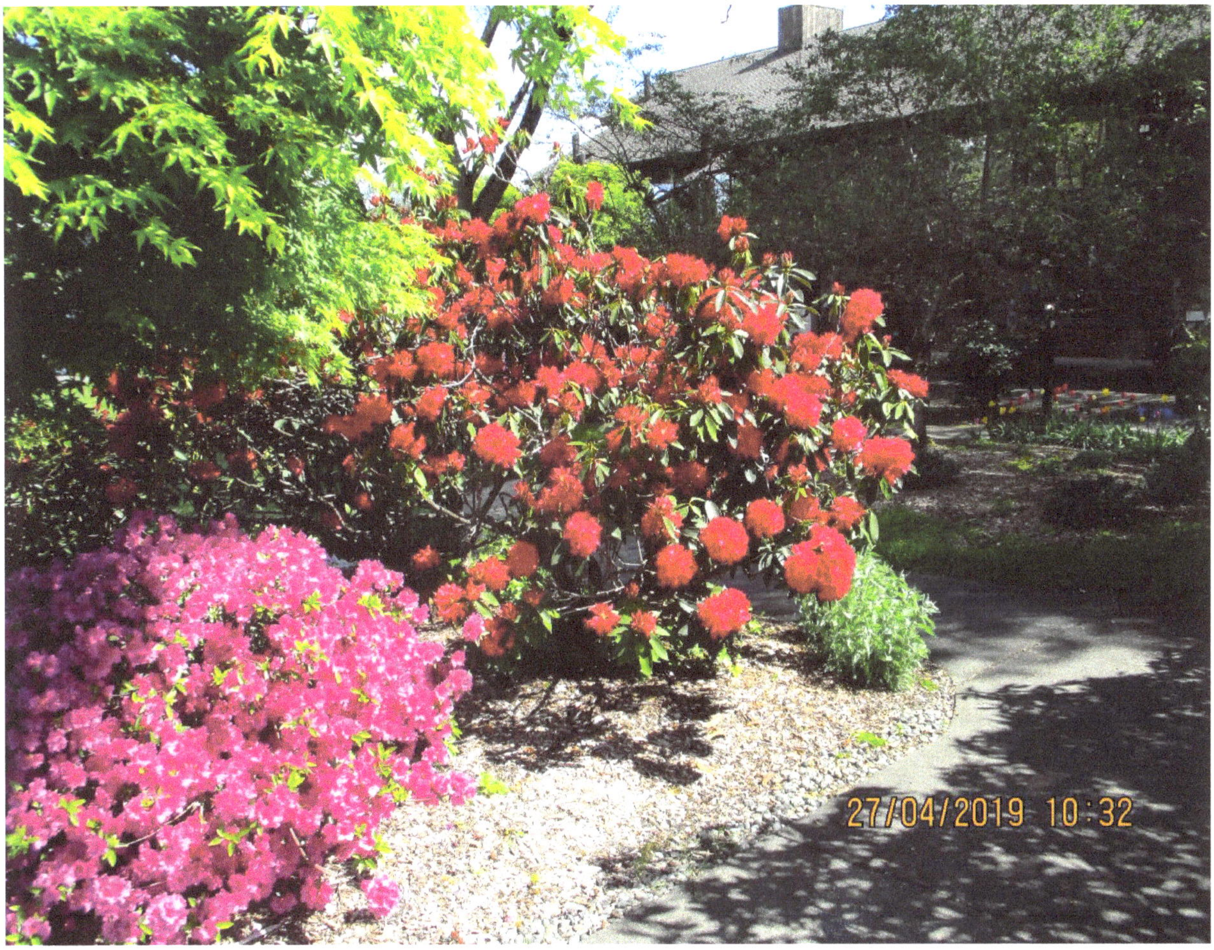
27/04/2019 10:32

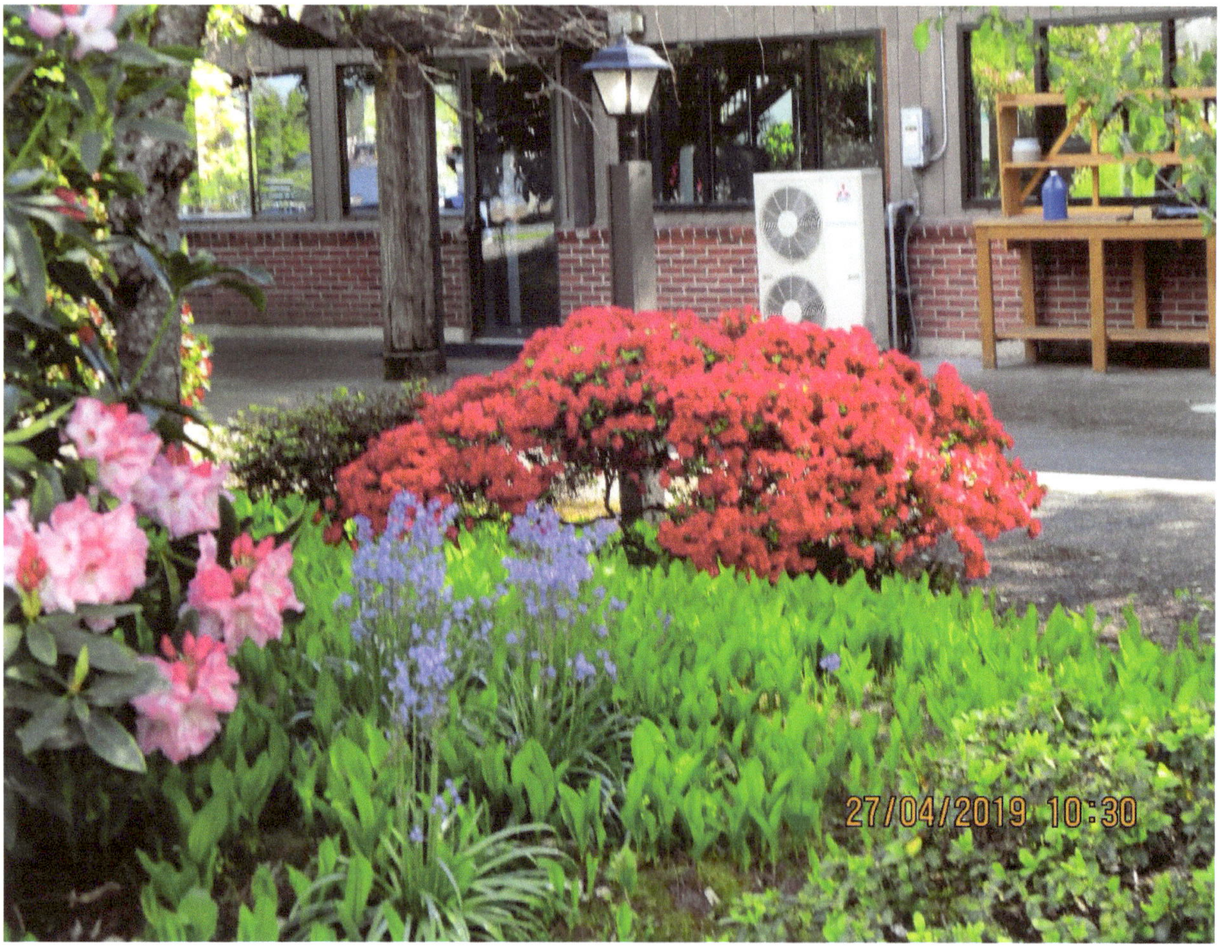
27/04/2019 10:30

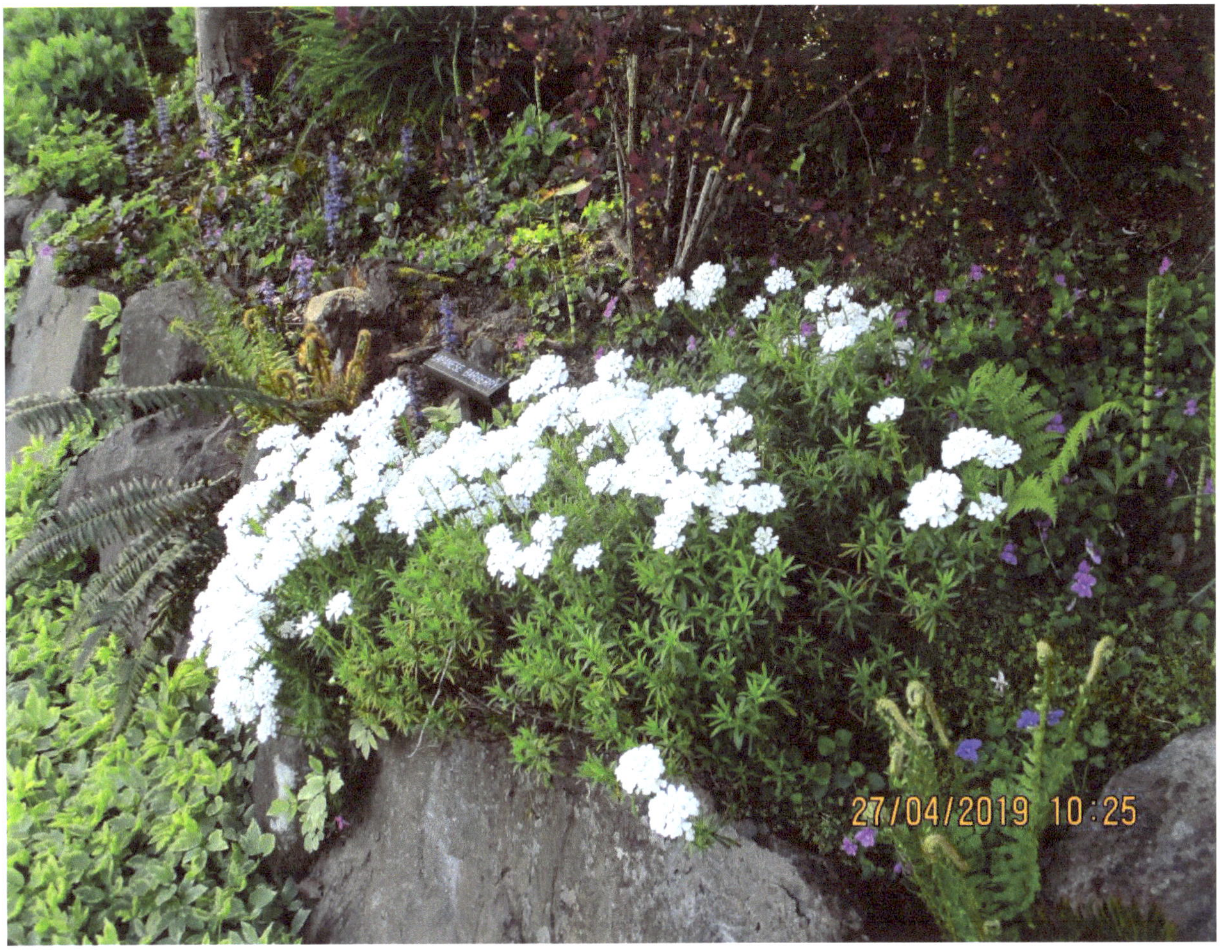
27/04/2019 10:25

* * *

That pretty much exhausts my collection of photographs. To be honest about it, there are many that I didn't think are good enough to appear here. Now, it's up to my publisher to preserve the colors as I have recorded them.

It's been a fun journey. Thanks for joining me.

About the author

John Sager is a retired United States intelligence officer whose services for the CIA, in various capacities, spanned more than a half-century. A widower, he makes his home in the Covenant Shores retirement community on Mercer Island, Washington.

©Yuen Lui Studio, 2003

CPSIA information can be obtained
at www.ICGtesting.com
Printed in the USA
BVHW022251150520
579758BV00001B/1